THE
I·N·D·O·O·R
GARDEN
BOOK

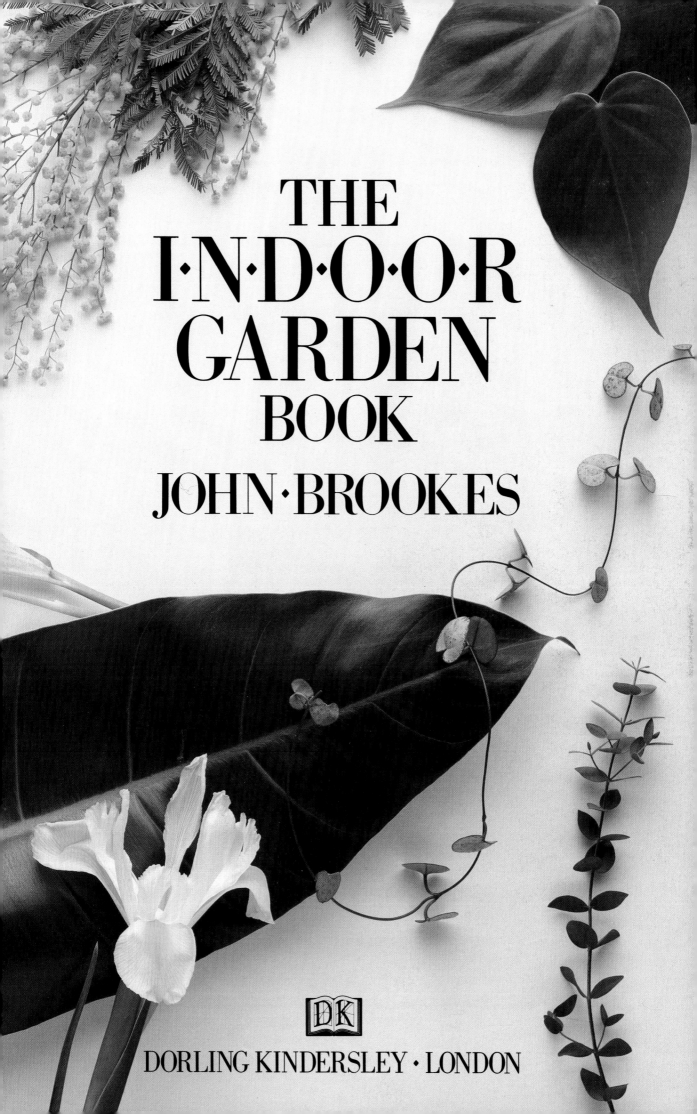

THE
I·N·D·O·O·R
GARDEN
BOOK

JOHN·BROOKES

DK

DORLING KINDERSLEY · LONDON

Consultant editor
Richard Gilbert

Project editor
Elizabeth Eyres

Art editor
Jane Owen

Editors
Sophie Mitchell/Tim Hammond

Designers
Cheryl Picthall/Ann Cannings

Art director
Anne-Marie Bulat

Editorial director
Alan Buckingham

First published in Great Britain in 1986
by Dorling Kindersley Publishers Limited,
9 Henrietta Street, London WC2E 8PS

British Library Cataloguing in Publication Data

Brookes, John
The indoor garden book: the complete guide to the creative use of
plants and flowers in the home.
1. House plants in interior decoration
I. Title
747'.98   SB419.25

ISBN 0-86318-172-4

Typesetting
Modern Text

Reproduction
Reprocolor International

Printed and bound in West
Germany by Mohndruck
Graphische Betriebe
GmbH, Gütersloh